NORMAN TIMES

KING WILLIAM

William the Conqueror had two great loves. One was his wife Matilda, who gave him nine children and helped rule Normandy when he was away. Matilda was only 1.26 metres tall (4' 2"). Was she smaller than you?

William's other love was hunting. He turned much of England into royal forests where no one but he and his friends could kill animals.

Two of William's sons were killed while hunting. One died in an accident but the other, William Rufus, was shot by an arrow. No one knows who fired it.

William was better at hunting than he was at writing. When he sent out a royal command and wanted to sign it, the best he could do was to mark a cross opposite his name.

The laws William made applied to everyone. He was often a harsh ruler, but he was as stern to Normans as to Saxons. Once he imprisoned his own brother, Bishop Odo, when he thought that Odo had disobeyed his wishes.

William encouraged the use of juries in trials and enquiries into crimes. A jury is a group of 12 ordinary people who have to decide if a prisoner is guilty or innocent. Juries had been used less often in England before William became king.

William took away the lands of English lords and gave them to his Norman followers. The Saxons looked upon them as foreigners. Later they would be accepted as overlords, but in the meantime the Norman nobles felt safer living in their wooden castles.

William also gave lands to the church. New monasteries for monks and nuns were built with beautiful abbey churches in the Norman style. The leaders of the monasteries, abbots and abbesses, were brought from Normandy.

Inside the monasteries, life was strict and hard. The day began at midnight with prayers in the abbey church. The monks—and in nunneries, the nuns—were woken from sleep by a bell.

The dormitories were near the church and a flight of stairs led down into it. These stairs, down which the monks filed in the darkness, can still be seen in some ruined abbeys.

The main meal of the day was served in a great hall called the "refectory". Talking was not allowed. During the meal one of the monks read from the bible, standing in a pulpit high above the tables.

Monks and nuns had to worship in the church eight times a day and they spent the rest of the time studying or in work about the monastery or in the fields. There were covered ways round open courtyards in monasteries, called "cloisters". Next to the cloisters there were little rooms where the monks wrote and copied books.

Many people were employed in the monasteries from outside. They worked in the kitchens, in the gardens and on the farms. The monasteries also gave work to stone masons, carpenters and other craftsmen working on the building of the great abbeys.

Some children were sent to monasteries to be educated and many stayed later to become monks or nuns. They were, however, only the children of nobles and rich merchants. Children from poor families did not go to school at all.

Later in his reign, William ordered a great survey to be made. He wanted to find out who owned everything so that Normans and Saxons could be taxed the proper amount. The details were written down in two volumes called the "Domesday Book".

William died before the book could be completed. Some people said that he had been a good king. Others said that he was a bad king. What do you think?

A SAXON VILLAGE in Norman Times

Some of the villagers are working in the lord's fields. Some are harvesting their own strips of land. Everybody is busy.

Problem picture

Study the picture and see if you can solve these problems:

1. A man is walking towards the stream. He has a sack on his back. What do you think he is carrying?

2. What are the two girls doing on the little hillock to the left of the picture?

3. Why are the two boys driving their pigs into the wood?

4. There is a large house in the background to the right of the picture. Who do you think would live there?

5. What is the building around which there are birds flying?

6. There are some men ploughing one of the fields. There is a boy with them. What do you think he is doing?

7. Two boys are running towards the stream. What is chasing them?

8. Why are the fields divided into narrow strips?

ARE THESE YOUR ANSWERS?

Here are the correct ones:

1

He is taking corn to be ground at the mill. Most villages had mills driven by water which were owned by the lord of the manor or the local monastery. Villagers had to pay for their corn to be ground and were not allowed to own a mill or grind their own corn.

2

The girls on the hillock are catching rabbits. One girl puts a fierce little ferret into one end of the warren and the other catches the rabbit in a net as it runs out to escape.

3

The boys are taking the pigs to feed in the wood. Pigs ate acorns and beechnuts. The woods belonged to the local lords or abbots who charged peasants for the right to run their pigs there. The rent they paid was called "pannage".

4

The large house belongs to the lord of the manor who owns all the land around. Many local Norman lords dug moats round their manor houses for the same reason that Norman barons built castles—for protection in case the Saxons turned against them.

5

The small building near the manor house is a dovecot. Doves were encouraged to roost and make nests in these special houses. Their eggs could be collected and some of the birds killed from time to time, for food.

6

The boy is using a sling to throw stones at birds to keep them away from the newly sown corn. Oxen were used to pull ploughs and harrows which were made of wood with iron tips.

7

The boys have overturned a beehive and angry bees are chasing them! Honey was important for there was no sugar for sweetening food.

8

The strips of land are where the villagers grow their crops. They rented the land from the lord of the manor but did not pay in money. Instead they worked a set number of days on the lord's land—sometimes as many as four days each week. They also gave part of their crops as rent.

HOW PEOPLE LIVED

There were no really big cities in Norman England. Cities are places for trade and there were few things to be bought and sold in shops in Norman times. The castles, monasteries and manor houses had their own bakeries, brewhouses, carpenters' shops and blacksmiths' forges. They grew all the food they required and did not need shops. There were small market towns where farmers could buy and sell. Most people, however, lived in the country and the next four pages tell what country-life was like.

Peasants lived in houses made of wood and mud. The walls were thin. One end of the long house was used for the family and the rest was for housing the cattle and storing hay.

Inside the house there was one large room. The fire in the middle of the earth floor was used for cooking and for warmth. There was no chimney and smoke just filtered out through the thatched roof.

If they were ill the peasants treated themselves with country herbs. If that did not cure them they could go to the monastery hospital (called the infirmary) where the monks or nuns might look after them. There were no proper doctors and operations were often done by barbers—without pain-killers!

Peasants hardly ever left their villages but if they had to go anywhere it was on foot. Carts were not used for travel. Ladies could either ride on horseback behind a servant or in a litter carried between two horses. Lords and knights travelled on horseback and goods were carried in packs tied to the backs of horses or mules.

4

The children of peasants had to work almost as soon as they could walk. But there were also times when they could play.

5

Hunting was the favourite pastime of castle folk. The king set aside a great area of forest where he and his friends could hunt but where it was forbidden for anyone else to carry bows and arrows or to run dogs. Norman lords could hunt on their own lands and they employed foresters to keep the peasants out.

6

One favourite way of hunting was with hawks. The sport was called "falconry" and every Norman lord and knight— and their ladies—possessed a hawk of some kind. It was "fashionable". The hawks were taken from their nest when very young and trained by skilful falconers to obey whistles and calls.

7

The hawks had tiny bells fitted to their legs so that they could be heard in flight and their heads were kept hooded when they were not hunting in order to keep them quiet.

CRIMES AND PUNISHMENTS

Although, in Norman times, juries were used in many trials, the ways in which some people were found innocent or guilty were still very unfair. Their punishments were also very cruel.

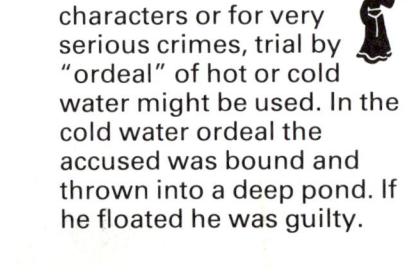

2

For those with bad characters or for very serious crimes, trial by "ordeal" of hot or cold water might be used. In the cold water ordeal the accused was bound and thrown into a deep pond. If he floated he was guilty.

1

When a person was brought before a Norman court of law accused of a crime, he might be allowed to prove his innocence by taking an oath before a church altar. Friends and neighbours might be made to swear that he had told the truth.

3

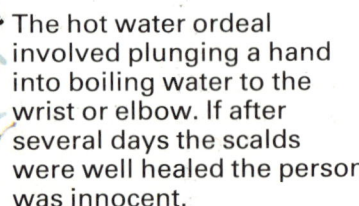

The hot water ordeal involved plunging a hand into boiling water to the wrist or elbow. If after several days the scalds were well healed the person was innocent.

Another ordeal was the carrying of a very hot iron a certain distance, the later healing of the burns deciding guilt or innocence. The idea behind trial by ordeal was that the decision was the judgement of God.